"Kim's story is
for a physician

Christopher T. Demas, MD
Director of Plastic, Reconstructive, and Hand Surgery
Staten Island University Hospital

"I couldn't put this book down. It was compelling to find out how much controversy Kim had to overcome in her life. I believe that writing is cathartic and Kim has accomplished a major step in taking back her life while sharing hope and strength with us—the readers. Kim is a survivor to the end—nothing will keep her down. I commend her for doing a great job and expect her to continue achieving success and happiness for the rest of her life."

JoAnn Fleming
Certified Public Accountant

"I was very impressed with Kim's book. It's not easy writing a book of any kind, but to write a book about the heartaches and tragedies in her life has to be even harder. I think anyone who reads this book will realize that life is not always fair and we are stronger than we give ourselves credit for. This book definitely proves that about Kim. As someone who was there for most of her ups and downs, I can say for sure that this book was written with absolute truth and endurance from her! I am proud that she had the strength and motivation to live through what she had dealt to her and still come out fighting."

Jan Steers
Nanny/Housekeeper

RINGS
AND
SHACKLES

Kim K. Forstater

Rings
And
Shackles

A Survivor Story

TATE PUBLISHING
AND **ENTERPRISES**, LLC

Rings and Shackles
Copyright © 2012 by Kim K. Forstater. All rights reserved.

No part of this publication may be reproduced, stored in a retrieval system or transmitted in any way by any means, electronic, mechanical, photocopy, recording or otherwise without the prior permission of the author except as provided by USA copyright law.

Scripture quotations marked "NIV" are taken from the *Holy Bible, New International Version* ®, Copyright © 1973, 1978, 1984 by International Bible Society. Used by permission of Zondervan Publishing House. All rights reserved.

Scripture quotations marked "Msg" are taken from *The Message*, Copyright © 1993, 1994, 1995, 1996, 2000, 2001, 2002. Used by permission of NavPress Publishing Group. All rights reserved.

Scripture quotations marked "CEV" are from the *Holy Bible; Contemporary English Version,* Copyright © 1995, Barclay M. Newman, ed., American Bible Society. Used by permission. All rights reserved.

The opinions expressed by the author are not necessarily those of Tate Publishing, LLC.

Published by Tate Publishing & Enterprises, LLC

---

127 E. Trade Center Terrace | Mustang, Oklahoma 73064 USA
1.888.361.9473 | www.tatepublishing.com

Tate Publishing is committed to excellence in the publishing industry. The company reflects the philosophy established by the founders, based on Psalm 68:11,

"The Lord gave the word and great was the company of those who published it."

Book design copyright © 2012 by Tate Publishing, LLC. All rights reserved.
Cover design by Allen Jomoc
Interior design by Jomar Ouano

Published in the United States of America

ISBN: 978-1-62024-823-2
Biography & Autobiography / Personal Memoirs
Self-Help / Personal Growth / General
12.08.16

DEDICATION

This book is dedicated to all my loved ones. My family members that are gone, you will never be forgotten. I love and miss you so much. A special thank you to my brother Dickie and his wife, Jan, for their love and support throughout the most difficult times of my life. I love you both very much. To my children, Patricia and Michael, you are my reason for living. I love you with all my heart. To my husband, Michael, thank you for convincing me to go on our first date and for not giving up. You showed me how to love again, and without you, I would not have my stepson, Jacob. I love you both so very much.

Table of Contents

Introduction 11

The Childhood No One Should Endure 13
Teenage Years and Fighting Tears 24
First Marriage: The Butcher Knife 39
Second Marriage: Broken Hearts 43
Third Marriage: First Love, Another Ring,
Some Bling, Only to Lose Everything 59
Single Mom for the First Time:
Shoot Me Please If I Ever Get Married Again 82
Fourth Marriage:
So Get Out the Gun and Shoot Me 87

Conclusion 97

Introduction

Just when you think everything is going to be okay, your life can fall apart in an instant. My life story is just that, about being okay and then falling apart and picking up the pieces over and over again. I've been told by so many people throughout my life that I should write a book. So here I am, doing just that, and I am letting people know that no matter how hard things might be, you will survive. I hope my story reaches out to those people who think life is just too much to handle and to let you know you're not alone. "I am a survivor, and you can be too." I hope my story touches you and, no matter what you are going through, it helps you get through it. I hope my story inspires you to keep fighting and never give up.

The Childhood No One Should Endure

Brooklyn, New York

My life began in Brooklyn, New York. I lived in Brooklyn until I was eleven with my mother and father and four other siblings. During the time I grew up, most parents stayed together no matter how good or bad their marriage might be. Well, up until I was about eight, I thought we were the average family until one night I saw my parents arguing. The arguing turned into my father beating my mother. At eight, I was the second oldest, and my older brother was only nine and a half. My two younger brothers were five and three, and my sister was just born. There was not much any of us could do except scream and cry to make him stop. My father was a raging alcoholic. He was verbally and physically abusive.

A short time later, we moved to an apartment building in Bay Ridge, where my father became the superintendent. It was a three-room apartment. There was one bedroom for all five children; a living room, where my parents slept on a pullout couch; and a small kitchen. The drinking got worse, and so did everything else. My father would go on his binges and take off for either days or sometimes weeks at a time. Sometimes I was glad he would disappear because there was no abuse. The only problem was that it left my mother in charge of taking care of the building. She could not do it with five children to take of, so my older brother and I would have to shovel the coal into the boiler and sweep and mop the halls, empty the trash bins, and clean up the laundry room. We were only nine and ten years old, not something children should be doing while all of our friends were out playing. But we did it because our mother needed the help.

Whether my father was gone for a day, a week, or a month, my mother always took him back. The abuse continued. I remember one day when I was ten, while I was in school, I got a bad feeling in my stomach. I felt something was wrong, and I wanted to go home. When I got home, I found the police dragging my father out of the apartment building with only one shoe on and his hands cuffed behind his back. I ran into the apartment to find my mother sitting at the kitchen table crying with sunglasses on.

"Mom, what happened? Why are you wearing sunglasses in the house?"

I reached over and took the glasses from her face to find two black eyes. We just sat there crying together.

"Mom, why do you keep going through this? Please stop taking him back."

"Kim, please don't worry. Everything will be okay."

"You always have the same answer, but it continues. As a matter of fact, it's getting worse and happening more. You know you are the only one who can make Daddy stop. Please, Mom, look at what he has done to you."

"Don't worry. It will be okay."

Staten Island, New York

Two years later we moved from Brooklyn to Staten Island into a bungalow with three bedrooms, a living room, a kitchen, and a dining room. Things started to look up. My father started going to AA meetings and got a regular job painting and wallpapering. I thought, *Wow, we are going to be okay.*

Well, I was wrong; it only lasted about seven months. This was the longest I ever saw my father sober until one day I came home from school and it was the same old story. This time my brother was involved. He was a teenager now and was starting to be able to take care of himself. He walked in while my father was beating my mother and tried to stop it. Then he and my father went at it. My older brother still wasn't strong enough. He got hurt, and my father ended up with stitches on his head from the baseball bat my mother hit him with. This was the beginning of my mother finally fighting back. Now her son was getting involved and hurt. Never touch a woman's child.

After that horrible day, my father disappeared again. We were left with no money and no food in the refrigerator. My mother had no job. Back then, mothers did not work; they stayed home with their kids. So she did what she had to and applied for welfare and food stamps. I was now in junior high school, and most of my friends' parents were together and not of the same background. I was so embarrassed, and obviously so was my mother. Even though we had food stamps for food, she was embarrassed to use them. She would always send me to the store to buy what we needed. I would always try to go to a store where no one I knew would shop just so they wouldn't see me using food stamps.

I am not sure how long it had been, but I hadn't seen my father for a while. My older brother and I were both in junior high, and my younger siblings were all in elementary school. That day I had come home from school, and to no one's surprise, my father was back home. Once again, my mother took him back. There was nothing any of us could do; it was her decision. Now we all knew it was only a matter of time before it would start all over again. My older brother and I had mutual friends and were always embarrassed to bring them home. We never knew what to expect, so why bother? By this time, everyone knew my father was the neighborhood drunk.

Rings and Shackles

Every day after school, I would come home to a bunch of chores. I would have to either cook, clean, do laundry, or babysit. Between school and my chores, I didn't have much time for my friends. It wasn't long before the drinking and fighting started again. My older brother and I just never wanted to be home anymore. We couldn't concentrate on our school work or anything else, for that matter. Most of all, we couldn't understand why our mother would continue to put all of us through this kind of life anymore.

After a few months, one morning I woke up to find out my older brother had not come home the night before. My mother was frantic, but I knew he was okay. He just didn't want to be there. Who could blame him? I figured he would be back. We had the same friends, and I figured he just stayed at a friend's house for the night. Another night passed, and he still wasn't home. I hadn't seen him for a couple of days, and none of our friends were talking. I just wanted to know if he was okay. One of our friends told me they knew where he was and not to worry. He had run away from home. So now I thought, *Wow, that's not a bad idea.*

So that night, when my parents were asleep, I did the same thing. I ran away from home to a friend's house a few blocks away. Both my parents started searching for us, but none of our friends would tell them where we were.

A week had gone by, and my parents were still searching for both of us, but no one was talking. Then one morning I woke up to find out that my brother had gone back home.

I thought maybe I should go back home too. I really didn't want to, so I didn't. Instead, my friends and I decided to go out in front of their house to hang out. Much to my surprise, my father pulled up in front of their house and dragged me into his car by my hair. He beat me all the way home.

When we got home, the beating continued with him beating me to the floor, at which point the punching turned into kicking me in the stomach and anywhere else he could. The whole time my mother just stood there crying. She never stopped him. I was begging her to make him stop, but she didn't. When he was ready to stop, he finally did. I couldn't believe he could do this to me, and he was sober. Worst of all, I couldn't believe my mother let him. After a few minutes, I heard my father on the phone. I couldn't hear what he was saying, but I wanted to know where my older brother was. I knew he came home, but he wasn't there. They wouldn't tell me. I would lie on my bed for the next hour, just crying and wishing I was dead.

A few minutes later, I heard the doorbell ring. My father answered it. I heard him say, "She's inside. Come in."

It was two police officers, a male and a female. I was petrified, thinking, *What is he doing?* The female officer told me to stand up and put my hands behind my back.

"Mom! Dad! Why are you doing this? I didn't do anything wrong! Where are they taking me? Where is my brother?"

"You are going to the same place your brother is," my dad said.

I was handcuffed and put into the back of the police car. I didn't know what to expect next, but I was about to find out what happened to my older brother.

As I sat in the back of the police car, I couldn't help thinking, *How could they do this to me and my brother? All we did was run away from an abusive situation.* I thought my mother would understand.

The officers took me down to the police station and placed me in a room by myself. The woman police officer asked if I was hungry as she took off the handcuffs. I was starving; I hadn't eaten all day. As she went to get me something to eat and drink, I sat on a chair at a desk. It was the only furniture in the room of nothing but four walls. She came back within minutes with a sandwich and soda. I asked what was going to happen to me, and she said I would be staying for a while. I was waiting for a guard to transport me.

"Transport to where?"

"Oh, you are going to a place where all troubled teens go."

"But I am not a troubled teen. I just wanted to get away from my alcoholic father." I couldn't take it anymore.

The night had passed, and it was now early the next morning. I was left locked in a room by myself all night. I heard footsteps coming my way, and sure enough, the door opened and a woman guard told me to stand up as she cuffed me again and took me outside to a van filled with other teens.

"Where are we going?"

"You'll see."

The ride seemed like it took forever. We finally pulled up to this huge fenced-in place that looked like a prison. It was a juvenile detention facility in the Bronx. It was prison.

I had no idea what was about to happen to me. I figured the best thing I could do was keep my mouth shut and do what they said.

We were all taken to an area where we had to take off all our clothes. If that wasn't bad enough, they had to search my body to make sure I wasn't hiding anything. I was mortified, and now I was really becoming angry with my parents. I didn't belong there, and neither did my brother. All we did was run away. Most of the teens were bad teens with a history of violence and belonged to gangs. The guards made everyone take a shower and put on what looked like prison uniforms. Then we were escorted by the guards to an elevator.

While we were in the elevator, a girl leaned over and whispered in my ear, "I am going to get you tonight while you are sleeping."

I leaned back and whispered in her ear, "Not if I get you first."

When we got off the elevator, she pushed me, and the guards grabbed her. She started fighting with them. I will never forget the look on her face when they picked her up and threw her back in the elevator as they were beating her with their night sticks. I never saw her again. The rest of us were escorted to rooms down a long hallway. Each room had a steel door with a small window. There were two beds and a toilet and sink in each one. My room was the last room down the hall on the left side.

The guard unlocked the door and told me this was my new home. "You will be allowed out at certain times during the day for meals, exercise, and recreation." My roommate was already there.

"Wow, you're a big girl," I said.

"Yes, I am," she answered. "Don't worry about anything. I've been in and out of this place so many times, and no one messes with me. No one will bother you because you're my roommate."

"This is my first time, so I don't really know how to feel or what to expect. I will tell you one thing, I'm glad I'm bunking with you."

Two days later, a guard came to my room. "Kim, get up and get dressed. You're due in court in an hour."

When we got there, they brought me into a private room, where they told me to have a seat. I didn't know what to expect. I just waited.

After a while, the door opened, and a court officer came in with my parents and a social worker. I was so mad and hurt that I didn't even look at them. We all just sat there, not saying a word. The social worker asked me if I was all right and if I was ready to go home.

"No, I'm not ready to go home." I would rather stay where I was than spend another minute at home with them. "Look at my father—that is one of the reasons I don't want to go home." He reached over and tried to grab me. "Get him off me!" I yelled. They escorted my father out of the room. A few minutes later, they came back in. My father was giving me dirty looks. He came over to whisper in my ear.

"Kim, you better keep your mouth shut and tell the judge you want to go home."

"Dad, at this moment, I truly hate you, but I will do what you say."

After court, we all went home. On the way there, all I heard was "You're grounded for a month. No friends, no out, nothing except school."

I didn't speak to either one of my parents for that whole month. I just went to school, came home, did my chores, and went to my room. I learned a valuable lesson and decided from that moment on that I would really concentrate on my studies and make something of myself. I knew I needed to do this to make a better life for myself and one day my own children. I knew I didn't have a choice for my life as a child, but I certainly did as an adult. I was going to be somebody, not the person my mother was. I didn't want to be a woman who had to depend on a man for anything. I was going to make sure of it.

TEENAGE YEARS AND FIGHTING TEARS

Being a teenager is hard enough, but coming from a dysfunctional home makes it even harder, especially for a girl. Everyone knows becoming a teenage girl is not easy. All those hormones start working, and you really have no idea what's going on. The only time I actually felt happy was when I was in school. I loved school. I had the best teachers in junior high. The work was easy for me. Most of the time I didn't even need to study; just paying attention in class was enough.

I made a lot of friends in junior high. Best of all, I met my first boyfriend. They call it "puppy love." What's that? Love is love! The first year we were together was great. I never wanted to be away from him. He treated me with kindness and respect. I felt like somebody really cared about me for the first time in my life. Teenage boys are so different than girls. They seem like they always have to prove something. Boys have to hang out with friends and do stupid things. That's when it all started.

Our second year together, I was so happy and thought everything between us was so wonderful. All of a sudden, we started spending less and less time together. He wanted to be with his friends more than me, or so he said. Oh, he was with his friends all right, and plenty of other girls too. He started drinking and doing drugs. Wow, what a slap in the face. All he wanted to do was party and nab every girl he could. I couldn't believe at fourteen I was becoming my mother. As if the drinking and drugs weren't bad enough, he was now cheating on me too. I was heartbroken, but I loved him so much. I stuck it out for that whole year, believing in all of his broken promises, until one day I caught him cheating on me with someone I knew. I knew then that I could not do this anymore. I was so broken hearted, but I knew I had to break up with him. I knew it would have only gotten worse. I was devastated, and so was he. I became very depressed. Now the one place I never wanted to be became the only place I stayed: home.

The next year the only time I left the house was to go school. I didn't want to go out with my friends or do anything. My first love breaking my heart left me so empty inside. I thought I would never get over him. All I did was cry for days at a time. I didn't want to be home, and at the same time, I didn't want to go out. I guess I just needed to go through a grieving process that finally came to an end.

Now I was fifteen and in high school. We had just moved again to another house on Staten Island. The house was the creepiest looking house I had ever seen. It looked like a haunted house on top of a hill. I never felt comfortable in it. It always felt like someone was watching us. At night when I went up and down the stairs, I always felt a breeze, as though someone was passing me. I could feel a presence but never see anyone. It was so spooky. Everyone always told me it was my imagination. To this day, I still believe that house is haunted.

After a while, I started going back out with my friends. We would all hang out in the old neighborhood. Sometimes I rode my bike there or even took the bus. Even though my first boyfriend and I had mutual friends, I hadn't seen him in a while until one night I was with my girlfriends, and he came up behind me.

"Kim, I really miss you."

"I've missed you too, but you're not going to break my heart again. I care, but at the same time, I really don't."

After that he tried to get back with me a few times, but I didn't give in. I still loved him, but I wasn't about to go through the pain again.

It was now almost the end of my sophomore year in high school. It was a beautiful day, so after school I decided to ride my bike to the old neighborhood to see my friends. We all went down to the handball courts like we did so many days. I started feeling like things were looking up. I decided to take a bike ride around the beach. As I was riding, a guy came out of nowhere on his bike right beside me. I had never seen him before, but he knew who I was. He was a mutual friend of my older brother and my first boyfriend. He was three years older than me, and he had a job and a car. I thought, *Wow, this could be good. Things are looking up.*

We started going out like most normal people would on actual dates, to the movies and dinner. It was great. He treated me like he really cared about me. He would pay for everything, buy me things, and send me flowers, the whole deal, and I was happy again—or so I thought.

The summer passed, and school started again. I had the option of taking a regular curriculum or going into the co-op program. I chose co-op. Now was my chance to start making plans for my future. In this type of program, you get to go to school for a week and then work for week. Since I was always good in math and typing, I decided to get a job that I could apply both skills. Now I was working, and I had a boyfriend who treated me right. All I needed was to have a happy family life. Unfortunately, that would never happen.

A short time later, I came home to find my father sitting on top of my mother on the couch, strangling her. Once again, he had been drinking, and it escalated from an argument to him almost killing her. None of my other siblings were home yet, and all I could think to do was grab him from behind and try to get him off. After a few minutes, he let go and started screaming and cursing at me.

All I wanted to do was help my mother up and make sure she was okay. Once again, almost blue, she said the same old thing, "Don't worry, I'm okay," as she sat up crying.

That dreadful day was during a school week for me. The weeks I had school were early days, and I would get home before my other siblings. Everything had calmed down, and my father did his usual and passed out. My mother would pretend like nothing ever happened; that way no one would ever know. Well, now it was after 3 p.m., and my two younger brothers, ages ten and twelve, would come home first. Then my younger sister, age seven. My older brother, now sixteen, had not come home after school. He came home later that night.

When he came in, we were already upstairs in our rooms. I didn't tell my younger siblings what happened, but I sure did tell my older brother. By now he had been lifting weights for three years, and I knew he was really strong. My father was still passed out, so that night my brother let it go. Usually my father's drinking sprees lasted anywhere from days to weeks to months, and just like me, he was older and sick and tired of it. I knew I wasn't strong enough to really defend my mother, but my older brother was.

A couple of weeks passed, and once again I came home to my parents arguing, upstairs this time. I ran up to make sure my mother was all right. Again, he was hitting her. I tried breaking it up, but this time I couldn't. I was screaming and crying and doing the best I could to stop him, but I couldn't. He kept pushing me out of the way and going back at my mother. I was frantic and ran downstairs to the call the police.

Just as I hit the bottom of the staircase, my older brother walked in the front door. I was screaming and crying. Before I could say anything, he heard my parents upstairs and ran up there. I ran behind him. They were in my older brother's room. He grabbed my father, turned him around, and gave him one shot right smack in the face. My father flew across the room into an open closet onto the floor. He told my father, "That will be the last time you ever put your hands on my mother."

That was the last time. The drinking didn't stop, but at least the abuse did. As long as my father would just come home and pass out, everyone seemed to be okay. After all, we couldn't make him leave; it was up to my mother.

We all seemed to be all right until one day in January of the following year. All of my brothers were upstairs fooling around like they always did—boy stuff, wrestling with each other. They all came downstairs, and my twelve-year-old brother said he didn't feel well and had bruises all over his arms and legs. We all thought that maybe it was just from wrestling too hard. My mother gave him some pain reliever, and we all went to bed.

The next morning he couldn't get up, and he was feeling even worse. So my parents took him to the doctor. The doctor put him in the hospital to run tests and keep him under observation. The tests finally came back, and we got the worst news ever: he was diagnosed with acute leukemia, a blood cancer. That is what caused his bruises.

The next ten months, my brother spent more time in the hospital than home, and so did my whole family. The chemo, the blood transfusions, the bone-marrow transplant. We were all heartbroken. My brother fought with all his might, and for twelve, he had the willpower of a bull. I remember on some of the days when he was feeling better, he would take his IV pole, use it as a skateboard, and go up and down the hallways of the hospital. All the doctors and nurses got a kick out of it.

Three weeks before ten months of his diagnosis, the doctors told my parents it was time to take him home. There was nothing else they could do, and it was only a matter of time. Just make him as comfortable as possible. Back then they didn't have the technology they do today. So he came home, spending most of his time in bed. I would spend time with him every day, reading and talking to him. At nighttime I would just lay in his bed, holding him until he fell asleep and praying he would wake up the next morning.

One day shy of three weeks of my brother coming home from the hospital, I came home from school and went up to check on him. He was asleep in his bed, so I went into my room. A few minutes later, I heard him crying and ran into his room. When I asked him if he was all right, he told me he didn't want to die. I started crying with him and told him he was not going anywhere. He finally stopped crying, and I told him I would be right back. I went in my room to get this huge black-and-white panda bear my boyfriend gave me. My brother loved it. I put it in bed with him, and we all lay there until he fell back to sleep.

That night I got a bad feeling in my stomach, so I went downstairs to talk to my mother.

"Mom, is it all right if I sleep over at my friend's house tonight? I can't be home tonight."

"Sure, Kim. Go have a good time."

At three o'clock in the morning, I was awakened by my friend's mother. "Kim, you have to get up. I will drive you home. Your brother was rushed to the hospital."

"I knew it. That's why I couldn't be there tonight. I couldn't take seeing him like that. I just knew tonight was going to be a bad night." When we got to my house, my uncle was there waiting to hear from my parents.

The hours waiting for my parents to come home seemed like days. I wanted to go and be by my brother's side, but they wouldn't let me. Then the front door finally opened, and my parents walked in crying.

"Mom, Dad, what happened?"

"Everyone, sit down on the couch," Dad said. "This morning your brother got up to go to the bathroom. He was very weak, but he still wouldn't let us help him. So I waited outside the bathroom for him to come out. I heard a *bang* and asked him if he was okay. When he didn't answer me, I broke open the door and found him passed out on the floor. He was bleeding from his head. He was so weak that he fell and hit his head when he tried to get up. You're mother called an ambulance, and we rushed him to the hospital."

"Dad, where is he?" I asked. "Is he going to be all right? When is he coming home?"

Then they told us the one thing no one wanted to hear: "Your brother can't come home. He passed away this morning."

It was one month before his thirteenth birthday. I just wanted to die. I wanted my brother back. My father sat next to me and handed me the Saint Jude medal my brother always wore.

"Your brother wanted you to have this and to let you know he loves you very much."

All I could do was cry. I couldn't believe I would never see my little brother again.

I had never been to a funeral before this, and no one expects their first funeral to be their brother's. I will never forget walking in the door where my brother was. It took me a long time to get to the casket. When I saw him lying there, the pain was unbearable. When I finally made it to the casket, I couldn't stop crying. I just wanted to wake him up and bring him home. But I couldn't. I just couldn't understand how God could let this happen. I just kept sobbing uncontrollably. I felt like my heart had been ripped out. I didn't know what to do, and no one could make me feel better. I just wanted my brother back. I was only fifteen and didn't care what anyone had to say, because I knew it wasn't going to bring him back. To this day, I still cry over losing my brother. I miss him so much. The pain never goes away, but over the years it does become less unbearable.

A couple of months passed, and I started to come out of my shell. I started concentrating on my school work, my job, and going back out. It was so hard to concentrate on anything, but I knew I had to go on. Sitting home depressed and crying wasn't going to bring him back. I needed to think of the good times we had together and know that someday we would meet again. He passed in October, and it was now December. I was turning sixteen this month, and while most girls my age look forward to having a sweet sixteen party, I really didn't want to celebrate anything. When the morning of my birthday came, no one even wished me a happy birthday, not even my parents. Everyone in my house completely forgot. I didn't say anything. I just went to school. I thought maybe my parents had something planned after school, or maybe they really did forget. It was understandable. No one wanted to celebrate anything.

When I came home from school, still nothing. That day my boyfriend was working, and he didn't get home until later that night. He called me to say happy birthday and that he made plans for the weekend to take me out. I went back up to my room and started crying. My mother came up and asked me what was wrong, and I replied the same as she always did: "I will be okay. Don't worry about it."

The next morning my mom woke me up for school and sat on bed crying. "Kim, I am so sorry I forgot your birthday."

"Mommy, it's okay. I understand." Well, I never had a sweet sixteen, but that weekend celebrated my birthday.

Christmas that year was hard on everyone. It just wasn't the same without my brother. We all missed him so much. My father was drinking even more now, and even I wanted to myself. I didn't, though; I kept up with school, work, and going out with my boyfriend. We all just did the best we could. Being in my junior year in high school, I knew I had to focus and do the best I could. During the course of the year, things seemed to be getting better.

On Memorial Day Weekend 1977, seven months from the passing of my brother, a lot of people went away. My younger brother, age eleven, was invited to go on a camping trip with his friend's family Upstate. My parents let him go. We were all sitting down for dinner and about to celebrate my father's and older brother's birthday when the phone rang. I got up to answer it.

"Hello. This is an officer from Upstate. May I please speak to your father?"

"Dad, it's a police officer from Upstate, and he wants to talk to you."

I will never forget the look on my father's face. He hung up the phone after speaking with the officer and sat back down.

"Dad, what's wrong?" I asked. "What did he want?"

"Listen, everyone, stay seated and calm," he started. "Something terrible has happened, and your mother and I have to leave and go Upstate. There was an accident, and your brother is in the hospital. We have to leave right now."

"What happened to my brother?"

"They wouldn't tell me everything, and we need to go right now." My uncle came over and stayed with us while my older brother and parents went to the hospital.

Once again, only seven months after my other brother's passing, I was sitting and waiting to find out what happened to another brother. It seemed like eternity. The phone call finally came. My uncle answered it this time—it was my father.

"There was a terrible accident. My son fell off a raft in the lake, and they couldn't find him for forty five minutes. When they finally did, the paramedics worked on him for a long time. They got a pulse and a heartbeat, and they rushed him to the hospital."

My brother would lay in a coma for three days. The doctors told my parents if he lived, he would be a vegetable for the rest of his life. He died on May 31, another brother in a seven-month period. I couldn't even begin to understand what was happening.

I was so heartbroken. In less than a year, I lost both my younger brothers. All I kept thinking was that this was God's way of punishing my father for all his sins, and one by one we would all be gone. I really don't know how I got through it, but I did. The priest told me there is a book written on all of us and only God knows when it is our time and that they were both together now, comforting each other in a better place. I truly started to believe that, because they were both angels and very young when they were taken away. They needed to be together in a safer place. I knew if I did believe that, it would help me cope and possibly make it easier to heal.

After a couple of weeks, I went back to school. I was still a junior in high school. My teachers told me I didn't even need to finish out the year and I should go back home. I told them I couldn't take being home anymore and wanted to keep busy. My teachers didn't have a clue as to what was going on at home.

At this point my father's drinking overcame him. That's all he did. Sometimes I told myself, "Who could blame him?" My mother, on the other hand, was taking prescription medication. My younger sister was still too young to know what was really happening. My older brother joined the navy, and I went to work and school. Nothing would ever be the same.

A short time after, we moved again to another area of Staten Island. It was now only my mother, father, sister, and me—a family of seven to a family of four. It was a small two-bedroom apartment. My sister and I bunked in one bedroom, and for the first time, my parents had their own bedroom. I was now seventeen and a senior in high school. I was hardly ever home anymore between work, school, and my boyfriend. I would come home to sleep, and that was about it. It was never the same, and I just couldn't wait to graduate and move on with my life.

Graduation finally came, and my father was nowhere to be found. He did his usual and disappeared for a while on yet another drinking spree. My mother, on the other hand, was there for me. She had even started working full time, earning her own money.

After graduation, I was offered a job in Manhattan. I started working full time immediately, and when September came, I started business school, studying accounting and business management at night. By now, my father was back in the picture. Once again, my mother took him back. At least this time, she didn't have to depend on him or public assistance for money. She was finally earning her own and learning to stand on her own two feet. Things seemed to be getting better again, and everyone was busy. My father even got a job as a boiler man.

The holidays were coming, and so was my birthday. After work on my birthday, my boyfriend picked me up at the ferry. I was so surprised. I asked him what he was doing there.

"It's a surprise. I am taking you out for your birthday."

He took me to a small Italian restaurant that we went to many times. It was one of my favorites. We had now been dating for almost four years.

After dinner, he got down on one knee. "Kim, I love you so much and want to spend the rest of my life with you. Will you marry me?

"Yes, yes. Of course, I will!"

It was one of the happiest days of my life. We had such a beautiful night. We decided to wait for a year before we would get married. I wanted to finish business school and get a better job. I finally had something wonderful to look forward to: planning my wedding.

For the next year, I continued my education at night and worked during the day. I saw my fiancé on the weekends. I didn't spend much time at home, only at night to sleep. When I was home, everything seemed to be all right. Both parents worked now, and when they were home, they seemed to get along. A while had passed again since my father's drinking. I am not sure how long, but it seemed the longest time I could remember.

Graduation came and went, and it was now time to start planning for my wedding, but first I wanted a better job. I started looking, and within a couple of weeks, I got one working as an assistant to the vice president of finance at a huge stock brokerage firm in Manhattan.

First Marriage: The Butcher Knife

I was now nineteen and would spend the next six months planning for my June wedding to a man that would turn out to be…the devil himself! Yes, I was about to marry the devil, and I didn't even know it until after I said "I do." I had a beautiful June wedding. Everything was perfect: the wedding, the reception, and even our wedding night. The night of our wedding, we stayed in a small hotel room and left the following morning for our honeymoon. Everything was so wonderful. We woke up and were on our way. We arrived in the early afternoon to a beautiful honeymoon suite, with the heart-shaped tub and all. We unpacked, spent some time in the room, and then decided to take a tour. It was so nice and filled with a lot of other honeymooners. After our tour, we decided to spend the rest of the afternoon in our suite with champagne, strawberries, and just the two of us. What could be better?

That evening we had dinner reservations with live entertainment—a DJ and a band. We danced, we ate, we drank. Then the DJ started picking couples from the audience to come onstage for some fun. He started picking couples. Yes, you guessed it. We were one of the couples. They asked all the couples to participate in some fun games, so we did. At first it was a lot of fun. Then one of the games was to pass an apple from under your chin down a long line of willing participants. When my husband passed the apple to me, it fell, and while everyone else was laughing and having a great time, to my unexpected surprise, he was furious. I couldn't believe my ears and eyes; I was so humiliated. He started yelling and calling me names. I said, "It is just a game. What's wrong with you?"

He called me stupid and grabbed me forcefully to leave. "Let's go. We are leaving now."

I couldn't believe it. As we rushed back to the room, all he did was scream and pull me the whole way.

The nightmare began. He unlocked the door and threw me into the room. He started smacking and pushing me to the floor. I kept begging him to stop, but he wouldn't. He threw me on the bed and told me to take my clothes off.

"Please stop it. You're hurting me! Leave me alone!"

"No, I'm your husband now, and you will do what I say."

He ripped my clothes off while smacking me and pulling my hair. Then he did the unthinkable—he raped me. I never thought you could be raped by your own husband. But it can happen, and he did. The beatings, rapes, and abuse continued for the next year and a half. I couldn't believe this was happening to me. How could this man turn out to be such an animal and I not know it before I married him?

I started to schedule my night classes in college at different times than him just so I didn't have to be around him. I wanted to leave him, and I needed to figure out how. I hadn't told my family what he was doing to me. I was too embarrassed. I just wanted to handle it on my own. Everything seemed to be fine for a while until one morning I woke up and, while I was taking a shower, I found a lump in my left breast. I made an appointment with the doctor, and after my tests and exam, I was told I needed surgery to remove it. I had the surgery, and it was a benign tumor. I stayed in the hospital for a few days and went home all bandaged and wrapped up. I was told to rest and not unwrap myself until I went back to the doctor.

After a couple of days passed, I got a call from my mother.

"We are having a seventy-fifth birthday party for your grandmother in a couple weeks."

"Oh, Mom. That's great. I would love to come." After I hung up the phone, I told my husband the plan. "Honey, my mom is having a party for my grandmother."

"Well, Kim, we aren't going. I don't want anything to do with your family. You're my wife, and you will do what I tell you."

"You don't have to go, but it's my family, and I'm going."

Then he started pushing me. He punched me right in the breast where my stitches were. At that moment, something inside me completely snapped. I went into the kitchen and took a butcher knife from the block. I ran after him like an animal chasing him through the house. He ran into the bathroom and locked the door as I stood outside of it screaming and stabbing the door. That would be the last time a man would ever physically abuse me. I was not going to suffer years of abuse like my mother did.

That night as he stayed locked in the bathroom, I packed up as much as I could and went to my mother's. A few days later, he called me, begging me to come home. I told him I would never be abused again. He was crying and told me he would change, but for me it was too late. I deserved so much more out of life and so much better. I waited a couple of weeks, and when I knew he left for work, I went back and packed up some more things and left for good. I filed for divorce and moved in with my mother. Yep, back home. The only difference was that my mother, after twenty five years, had finally had enough of my father, and she divorced him. I saw my husband one time after that at the divorce hearing, and then I never saw him again.

Second Marriage: Broken Hearts

I quit my job in Manhattan and started looking for something else. I just wanted to start a new life, and that meant changing everything. I found a job in New Jersey doing accounting and administrative work at an electric motor company. While I was there, I met someone. He was the maintenance manager. At first, of course, we were friends. He was married and had a six-year-old daughter.

While working there, one of the other employees collected money each week for lottery tickets.

"Hey, Kim. You hit four numbers and won some money."

"Oh my God, that's great! How much did I win?"

"I'm not sure. You have to take it to the store and find out."

I was so excited, and when he gave it to me. My friend was there and asked me what I was going to do with my winnings. I said I didn't know, and then he said, "Why don't you take me out to lunch?"

I said, "Why not?" I didn't think there was any harm in it; we were just friends. So we went to lunch and had a great time. He told me about his marriage, and I told him about mine.

Months passed, and he was so unhappy with his life too that he decided to end his twelve-year marriage. We started dating. I also decided to leave my job, because I didn't think it was a good idea to work together. He was a great man and made me feel loved again. We moved in together a short time later, renting an apartment in New Jersey. I also got a new job as an accounting manager at a moving and storage company. Everything in my life started falling into place, and I felt alive again.

We lived in the apartment for a year and decided to buy a house. He asked me to marry him, but I said, "Why ruin a good thing? Let's just live to together, and maybe down the road we'll get married."

So that's what we did. We bought a house—a small handyman special in Central Jersey—and spent the next couple of years renovating it.

About three years into our relationship, I began feeling like something was missing. Here I was with a great man who treated me well. At that time I couldn't say one single negative thing about him. When he asked me to marry him again, I decided to talk with him about it. We talked about everything, and when we got on the subject of children, he told me he had one and didn't want any more. After his daughter was born, he had a vasectomy.

I knew throughout our relationship that more children weren't in the picture for him. At the time I was twenty-three and knew I wasn't ready for kids yet, but I wanted them in the future. I told him that when I was ready to have children, I would do it with or without him. If he could handle that, then I would marry him. He agreed to it, and we got married October 1984.

Our wedding was small and simple in our backyard. It was wonderful, and we had a great time with our families and close friends. He also decided to leave his job and take one closer to home. It was a great job for him and, in the beginning, for us. The longer he was at this job, the more customers requested him, which meant he needed to travel. At first the traveling wasn't too bad, but after a while, more and more customers requested him, and over the years, he was gone a lot. I worked a lot too, so I was busy myself. When he came home, we spent a lot of quality time together.

The years passed, and I still felt like something was missing. It was now 1988, and I started thinking about my biological clock ticking. My husband and I sat down to talk.

"Honey, in two years, I will turn thirty, and I want to have a baby or at least be pregnant by then."

He agreed we would to go to the doctor to see if his vasectomy could be reversed. So we did, and we left the doctor's office with a disappointing *no*. We discussed what our options were at the time, and I really didn't know what to do. I wanted my husband's baby, not some stranger's.

Shortly after getting the bad news, I talked to my sister-in-law about it, and she looked at me and gave me a hug. She then said something I never thought anyone would ever say to me: "Why don't we have my husband donate his sperm?"

This was the wife of my husband's younger brother. I started to cry and couldn't believe someone would do that for me. It was the most generous, selfless, and wonderful thing anyone had offered to do for me—ever. She went home and discussed it with her husband, and I with mine. Everyone agreed to do it. I couldn't believe it was going to happen. It was one of the happiest days of my life.

I called my gynecologist and made an appointed for a checkup and to discuss my options. He told me I could have artificial insemination and we could start whenever I was ready. Naturally, I was ready right away. He told me to get an ovulation kit and follow the instructions. So, of course, when I left the doctor's office, I went right to the pharmacy and picked one up.

Every month during the ovulation time, I had to go to my brother-in-law's house and pick up my donation in a baby jar, hold it under my armpit (the warmest part of the body), and make it to my doctor's office in two hours. If I didn't make it in time, the sperm would die. When I got there, he would do the insemination, and I would have to lie there for about an hour to give the sperm time to swim. I did this for the next year and a half without getting pregnant. I bought so many pregnancy kits that I could have had my own pharmacy. It was a huge disappointment, and I became discouraged. I thought maybe I was being punished for waiting so long to have a child.

Between visits, I went to see my doctor and to decide on what to do, because it wasn't working. He told me a new doctor—a specialist in this area—just opened his practice in South Jersey. I made an appointment, and my husband and I went. He examined me and ran some tests, which turned out to be fine. He said in order to know what was wrong, he wanted me to call when it was time for my next donation and he would take me right away.

When the time came, my donation and I rushed to his office. Time was an issue, and he took me in immediately. At first he did the artificial insemination and waited about fifteen minutes. He then took samples from my uterus, and there was no sperm there; they all died in my cervix. The poor babies never had a chance to swim.

"Don't worry. There is another way," the doctor informed me. "It's called inter-uterine insemination. I will bypass the cervix and go right the uterus." So with the sperm that was left, that's exactly what he did. Then he told me, "Don't you worry. It will happen. I promise. Just be patient and try to relax and keep stress-free."

Yeah, right! We all know how hard that this.

The next six months, I went to the specialist and then took my pregnancy test, only to be disappointed month after month. My husband had a trip to Las Vegas in December 1990 for a show that his company went to every year. That year all the wives joined their husbands for a week's vacation. It was also a little more than a week before my thirtieth birthday, so I figured, what better way to celebrate?

It was my first trip to Las Vegas, and I was so excited. Before we left to meet our husbands, it was my time to see the doctor, and I had decided it would be the last time I would try. It was two years since I started the process, and after being through it all, I was going to give up. I wanted to be pregnant by my thirtieth birthday, and after two years of trying, it just seemed like it wasn't meant to be. I didn't even take a pregnancy kit with me.

During my flight, I did a lot of thinking and decided not to be upset anymore. I wanted to have a good time, and I had not seen my husband for a couple of weeks. We were with our friends, and I just wanted to have a great time and enjoy the trip. So that's exactly what I did.

A few days into my vacation, I started feeling sick. I thought I caught some kind of stomach virus. I still had a great time and just excused myself when I had to. We saw shows, went shopping and out to dinner, and we just really enjoyed ourselves. The week was over, and it was time for the wives to go home. All the husbands had to stay for a few more days.

My husband came home for my birthday, and we went out to dinner with some friends. Shortly after we got home, my stomach started bothering me again, and I had to run to the bathroom. I started thinking maybe it was not a virus, so I took out one of my pregnancy tests. When I came out of the bathroom, my husband was standing there waiting.

"Babe, are you okay?"

"It's my stomach again. I took a pregnancy test, and we need to wait ten minutes." We waited, and honestly I was afraid to go back in the bathroom to check it. I just paced back and forth for a while.

After about a half hour, I went in and looked. I sat down for a couple of minutes because I just couldn't believe my eyes. I was pregnant and found out right on my thirtieth birthday. I came out and told my husband we were having a baby. You should have seen the look on his face. Neither one of us could believe it; it was a miracle. God did this. It was the happiest day of my life.

The next day I made an appointment to see my doctor to confirm the results. After testing me, he congratulated us with a big smile on his face. "I told you it would happen."

I was so happy and couldn't wait to tell everyone. After two years I was finally having a baby. Everyone was so happy for us too. It was the best feeling in the world, and it was a true miracle.

For the first two trimesters, my pregnancy wasn't bad at all. It was pretty normal with no complications, except for gaining a lot of weight. I was six months and had already gained forty pounds. The third trimester, I started having some health issues. I developed gestational diabetes, carpel tunnel syndrome, tendonitis, and a blockage in my sinus cavity. There was nothing any of my doctors could do because I was pregnant. I had to wait until after I gave birth to fix my health issues, and I didn't mind either. I just wanted a healthy baby. During my last trimester, I packed on another twenty pounds, for a total of sixty.

During the last month, I had to go the hospital a few times for Braxton-Hicks contractions. They were brought on from dehydration, even though I was drinking one hundred ounces of water a day. I couldn't hold the water during the last month. My baby was due September 4, 1991, which came and went. Everybody knows it's never an exact date, so I wasn't worried, and during that time I saw the doctor every week anyway. So when I went for my checkup the next day, my doctor was concerned.

"Kim, if you don't go into labor on your own, I will need to induce. Your health is getting worse, and we really can't wait any longer." He then scheduled me to induce labor on September 11.

On the evening of September 10, I was packed and ready to be at the hospital for 7 a.m. the next morning. It was around 10 p.m., when my husband went to bed.

Rings and Shackles

I stayed in the den on my recliner watching television, because I just couldn't sleep. I was so big, and I couldn't get comfortable. Around midnight I started getting pains and was sitting there thinking, *Here I go again with the Braxton-Hicks contractions.* I kept watching television, and then about twenty minutes later, it started again. So I started watching the clock for the next three hours. Over that time, the contractions became stronger and were a lot closer. They were ten minutes apart. So I went upstairs and woke up my husband. He thought I was waking him for my 7 a.m. appointment.

"No, honey, we need to go. I'm in labor." I told him I was going to take a shower and then we would leave. By the time I was out of the shower, the contractions were eight minutes apart.

The hospital was twenty minutes from our house. By the time we got there, my contractions were four minutes apart. They took me up to labor and delivery, and they became two minutes apart. Then, of course, one minute to no minutes. I was fully dilated, and it was time to push. I pushed for hours and couldn't push the baby out. They cut me from one end to the other and still couldn't get my baby out. The baby's heart rate kept dropping, and it turned out that the umbilical cord was wrapped around the neck and the baby was turned the wrong way.

After everything it took to have this baby, I started crying and telling my doctor, "Please, you have to get my baby out."

He started turning the baby around inside me, and when he was done, he told me to start pushing again. He got a pair of forceps and a plunger and began pulling my baby out. At 9:04 a.m. on September 11, 1991, my daughter was born. She was beautiful, with red hair and blue eyes.

It was the happiest day of my life. My poor baby, though, had a broken collarbone, and her little nose was smooched to one side from all the pushing I did. She came out face up instead of crowning properly. This created a problem where the nurses couldn't get all the mucus out, and she kept choking on her own saliva. I would have to suction it out for months after her birth. She would choke on her formula all the time. As far as the collarbone, they said it would heal on its own. Because she was a baby, all her bones were soft and would heal by themselves.

My in-laws, of course, were just as happy as I was. They were also her godparents. This was the agreement we made because of what they did for us. They would have been the godparents no matter what. We had ten years to become close, and I loved them both very much. I am eternally grateful to them both.

Six weeks later, we had the christening with our families and friends. Everything was as perfect as it could be. I never thought I could be so happy. This was what life was all about. I felt like I was on top of the world, and nothing could take that feeling away.

After the christening, I scheduled all my doctor appointments for my health issues. I needed surgery for everything except the gestational diabetes, which went away after giving birth. So I had the surgeries, and everything turned out fine. The sinus blockage turned out to be a tumor behind my eye socket. They took it out, and it was benign.

Everything was wonderful. My husband seemed to be around more. He cut back on his traveling, and we were one big happy family. My daughter was now seven months old, healthy and happy. I never wanted to be without her. I even tried bringing her to work, but it was just too much lugging everything she needed back and forth. So I decided and work agreed for me to stay home. When they needed me, I would work out of the house. Life was just perfect—a little too perfect. I was always waiting for that bomb to drop. That's just the way my life was. Whenever I was happy, something horrible would always take that happiness away.

On April 16, 1992, Holy Thursday, Easter weekend, my phone rang. It was an aunt of mine that I hadn't heard from in a while.

"Kim, I have some really bad news. Your mother was in a horrible accident and had to be flown by helicopter to a hospital Upstate."

I called my friend across the street to take my daughter, and my husband and I got in the car and started driving for hours.

When we got to the hospital, my brother was there, pacing back and forth in front of the door. Even the look on his face couldn't prepare me for what I would see behind that door. We hugged.

"Kim, it's really bad. She's down the hall."

The hallway down to the room where she was seemed miles long. When I got to the room, I saw my mother lying on a table, with blood-soaked bandages wrapped around her head. Her head looked like a large pumpkin from the swelling. Every part of her body was swollen. I stood there just sobbing and praying. It was the worst thing I had ever seen in my life.

A few minutes later, my husband came in. He didn't say a word and just held me. Then the doctors came in and gathered the rest of my family. They said she was getting onto the highway and was hit by a tractor trailer. She had massive head trauma, and her heart stopped several times. They were keeping her alive with the machines. If she were to live, she would be a vegetable. We all looked at each other and then looked at the doctor in disbelief.

My brother said, "What are you saying? My mother's gone and there's nothing we can do about it?"

The doctor said he was so sorry, but we needed to make a decision.

Again, we looked at each other and said at the same time, "Don't pull the plug." How could they even ask us to do that? We all spent the next twenty-two hours going back and forth, not even really talking to each other. What were we going to say when we all felt the same pain?

The waiting seemed like forever. We all knew what was going to happen, but we just waited. We were all sitting in the waiting room when the doctors came out and told us my mother's heart stopped and they couldn't revive her. It was Friday, April 17, 1992, Good Friday. We all just started crying again. They told us to stay where we were and that they would be back in a few minutes. They were going to move her to a private room where we could say our good-byes. My mom was only fifty-two years old.

We all went into the room by ourselves, one at time. My husband came in with me. It was very hard to say good-bye, and all I did was cry.

I spent the next year in a deep depression. I stopped going out. I didn't want to socialize at all, with family, friends—just no one. My daughter became my rock. Without her, I would have never gotten through it. Just knowing she depended on me and to see her smile every day helped me get through it. The way I grew up, I had a lot of resentment for my mother, and we had a lot of unresolved issues. She never even knew my daughter. We weren't close, but I still loved her very much. After she died, I knew in my heart that I would make sure I was close to my children. I would be there for them no matter what and wanted them to know they could always come to me about anything.

After losing my mother, I decided to start searching for my father. After their divorce, my father disappeared. I hadn't seen him in twelve years. I didn't even care anymore about the horrible life we had. I just wanted to find him. I wasn't a kid anymore, and he was still my father. He was a Vietnam veteran receiving a pension. So I figured the best way to start was to get in touch with the Coast Guard pension division. It took me another year, but I found him in a hospital's cardiac care unit. He had suffered a heart attack three weeks earlier and had a triple bypass. He was three thousand miles away, so I talked to his doctors and him. My father was a drifter, an alcoholic, smoked four packs of cigarettes a day, and just lived an unhealthy life. When he recovered, I flew him back to live with me. He did great for the first year. He ate healthily, didn't drink, and spent a lot of time with my daughter and me.

One afternoon, he told me he was going to the store and that he'd be right back. Hours had passed, and he didn't come home. The day turned into night. I put my daughter to bed and went into the living room when I saw a police car in front of my house. I opened the door to see my father in the backseat.

"Hi. Are you Kim?"

"Yes, Officer. Why is my father in the back of your police car?"

"Well, to be honest, this isn't the first time we picked him up. It's the third time, and we told him we would have to tell you this time. We found him passed out in front of the neighborhood preschool."

I couldn't believe it, because I truly thought that being with his family and after what happened to him the year before would have changed him. For the next year it continued to get worse. I had to ask him to leave, and it broke my heart. But I needed to worry about my daughter; I didn't want her to live my childhood. I asked him to pack his bags and I would bring him to the airport. When we got there, I hugged him, told him I loved him, and said my good-byes.

During that time, and for a few years after, my husband opened his own service company, and I opened my own retail business. He started traveling a lot again, and I felt very alone. I didn't want to put my daughter in daycare, so by opening my own store, she would be with me all the time. I was pretty much a single mom, and I started falling out of love with my husband. I knew I wanted more children, and he didn't. What was I going to do to have more children? According to my doctors, I couldn't have them the normal way, and I wasn't about to ask my brother-in-law. I didn't want my daughter to grow up an only child. I wanted a house full of kids.

I kept going back and forth in my head, not knowing what to do. I was becoming more and more unhappy every day. He didn't do anything wrong, but I just couldn't live a lie anymore. I fell out of love. Years later I realized that I was never truly in love with him. I loved him dearly, but I wasn't in love with him. He was twelve years older than me and was a wonderful husband. But we didn't share the same values in life, and I just couldn't do it anymore.

A few months before I ended my marriage, my sister called me to tell me she saw my first love—the one who broke my heart and I never forgot about. She gave me his phone number, and I waited about a week and called him. We spent the next three weeks talking on the phone. He told me he gave up everything and he was working and living alone. He never fell in love after me, and I was the only woman he ever loved.

We decided to meet. He still lived in the same house. My sister and I drove there, and he was waiting outside. I will never forget the look on his face when I got out of the car. It was like twenty years had stood still. I knew then that I really couldn't stay married. I divorced my husband shortly after. I broke his heart, and I spent many years being sorry for it. But I knew if I stayed with him, I would end up hating him. He didn't deserve that.

Third Marriage:
First Love, Another Ring,
Some Bling, Only to Lose Everything

I ended up back with my first love. We got married in 1996—a year later. Our first year together was perfect. Our love for each other had never died. Throughout my life, I always said something was missing. I thought that something was him. I felt complete for the first time in my life.

In January 1997, my sister-in-law came over to give me the horrible news.

"Kim, I am so sorry, but I just got a phone call asking for your brother, and since he was at work, I took the call. The man on the phone said he found your father on the floor of the room he was renting. He suffered another heart attack and passed away." He was fifty-seven.

She gave me the number, and I called and made the arrangements to have him flown back home. Regardless of my childhood, and even part of my adult life, I couldn't leave him. I knew the right thing to do was to bring him back and give him the military funeral he should have.

My father dying was a lot harder for me than I thought it would be. At first I thought maybe he would finally be at peace, but then I knew most of family was gone, and all that was left was my older brother, younger sister, and me. We went from a family of seven to a family of three. But I also knew I needed to go through the grieving process and continue with my life. Having my own family really helped, especially my daughter. Loving her and waking up to her beautiful face every morning really helped me get through so many things.

My husband was working, and since we were together, I was a stay-at-home mom. He had two tumors on his body that needed to be removed. So we made an appointment for surgery, and he had to stay home for about a month after it. His boss let him go during his time out, which meant we had no income coming in. So I went back to work as a controller for a direct mail and marketing company in Manhattan, and he became a stay-at-home dad. I didn't want my daughter raised by anyone else.

Not long after starting my new job, I noticed a change in my husband. I became suspicious of what he was doing all day while I was at work. One night I was putting laundry away and found a controlled substance in one of his drawers. I confronted him.

"What is this? What have you been doing?"

"Honey, I swear it's not mine. I'm holding it for someone because he didn't want his wife to find it."

"I don't believe a word you're telling me. Now take it and flush it down the toilet."

I felt like my life went backward in time to over twenty years before. Now I knew I couldn't trust him again, just like when we were kids.

"I don't believe you, and if it doesn't stop, one day you will be very sorry. I will leave you for good."

A few months passed, and things were going well at my job and at home. One day I woke up not feeling well and had to run to the bathroom. I thought I had a stomach virus or something. It continued for days, and I started feeling really sick and fatigued. So I went to the hospital with my sister-in-law, and they asked me if I could be pregnant. Of course I said that was impossible and that I could only have a child if I went through the insemination process. He suggested I do a pregnancy test anyway. So I did and got the surprise of my life. Yep, I was pregnant with my second child. It was crazy. I was one of those people you hear about all the time who couldn't have kids, and then they were pregnant when they least expected it. I was thirty-seven years old, and I had started early menopause at thirty-five, so my child was a change-of-life baby. It was so amazing.

My daughter was six years old and was asking for a little brother, and here I was, having a baby. We were all so happy, and so were the rest of our families. Because I was over thirty-five, a few months later, I went for the amnio test. The results came in, and my daughter got her wish—a little brother.

I continued working and had a normal pregnancy with the exception of having gestational diabetes again. It made me very dehydrated, so I was at the hospital a lot for it. No matter how much water I drank, I still got dehydrated. During my last trimester, just like with my daughter, I had the Braxton-Hicks contractions. I would go to the emergency room all the time and have to be hydrated through IV. My due date was originally April 25, my husband's birthday, but of course I wasn't on time. I woke up at 3 a.m. on May 6 with contractions, stood up, and my water broke. I remember my husband yelling, "Yes, finally!"

I went and sat in the bathroom, and my husband called my sister and sister-in-law to come and get my daughter because I was in labor. They rushed over and came in the bathroom. They said, "Why are you still sitting there?"

"I have time. The contractions aren't too bad yet. They are still ten minutes apart."

I waited about an hour, until they were six minutes apart, and my husband and I went to the emergency room. At 10:35 a.m., I gave birth to a beautiful baby boy, named after his father. Right after birth, I decided to have my tubes tied. I had my boy and girl, and due to early menopause, I felt it was best.

It was time to go home to our small bungalow on Staten Island. It was the house my husband grew up in with six other siblings. The houses our families always lived in were too small, but we made do. What choice did we really have back then? I stayed home for a few more days before returning to work. I felt so good and happy about my life. I had a great job, everyone was doing well, and my family was complete.

The following week, I went back to work, and my husband stayed home with the kids. My daughter was in school all day, so he didn't really have much to do for her. But he had a new baby to take care of, his first and only son. I have to say, for the most part, he really did a good job taking care of him. Of course, when I came home from work, I would take over. But that was one thing I was proud of him for.

The next couple of years, we had our ups and downs, like any other marriage. I was busy all day working, and my husband was busy all day with the kids and renovating our house. My in-laws had still owned the house, so we bought it from them. I spent the next couple of years paying it off.

It was now October 2000, and I was thirty-nine years old. I woke up and was getting ready for work. I wasn't feeling too well and went to the bathroom. I was getting really bad pains in my stomach—not gas pains, really sharp, stabbing pains. When I sat on the toilet, I felt like I had to go, but all blood came out of my rectum. Most people probably would have panicked, but I didn't. I called my husband to come in, and I told him I needed to go to the emergency room. He freaked out more than I did.

When we got to the emergency room, they started running tests. They ended up admitting me. I spent the next two months in the hospital. I was diagnosed with diverticulitis, which I had never heard of. It's an intestinal disorder usually caused by stress. I had five tumors in my intestines and one burst, causing an infection throughout my intestines. The infection was spreading throughout my organs, and I needed IV antibiotics to clear it up before anything could be done.

After it cleared up, they cleaned out all of the adhesions left behind, and I was able to go home. After a couple days being home, my job needed me back to work, but I needed another couple of weeks to recover. So I decided it was a good time to stop working for someone and start my own accounting and bookkeeping business. I spent the next couple of years getting new clients and servicing the New York and New Jersey area. I did very well and was happy having my own business.

This was a good time in my life, and we needed a bigger house in a better neighborhood. So we put the house up for sale and moved back to New Jersey. We bought a Cape Cod fixer-upper in central New Jersey. It had a nice piece of property for the kids to play and for us to just relax and start enjoying our lives. We repainted, put down new carpeting, and made it comfortable. That was good enough for now until I saved some money to really make the house the way I wanted.

Two years later, in 2002, I started having more health problems. I got a terrible rash that started on my scalp and spread all over. I went to several doctors who told me it was an allergic reaction. They put me on cortisone medicine, pills, creams, and whatever else they could think of. Nothing seemed to work. I even went to a hospital in NYC for cancer and skin diseases. After months of tests, they said the same thing: it was an allergic reaction to chemicals, cleansing products, etc. The medicine I was on made me gain so much weight, and it didn't even help. It was so itchy that I was ripping my skin apart. I had to go for cortisone shots at the hospital—it was that bad. Then one day I was over at my brother's for a party, and my sister-in-law gave me the name of my niece's dermatologist. So I figured, what the heck; I had tried everything else.

I went a few days later. It was during the summer, so I was wearing a tank top. When I went in and started explaining what I was going through for the past year, she stopped me and said, "Forget about the rash. I need to examine your arm."

"Why my arm?"

"Kim, how long have you had that beauty mark on your arm?

"Since I was born, why?"

The next few words that came out of her mouth really took me by surprise. She said, "I'm pretty sure you have melanoma, skin cancer. I need to take a biopsy immediately," and she did.

Waiting for the results seemed like eternity. But she was right; I had melanoma. She called me with the results and told me I needed to see a surgeon immediately. So she recommended one, and that's exactly what I did. I had my surgery, which went well. My surgeon took a good margin around it and got everything. Because it was on my upper arm, the recovery was good and didn't stop me from doing things.

The next couple of years were pretty normal; the kids were getting older, my husband and I were okay, and even my business was doing well. What was great about my business was that I made my own hours, and I even made an office in my house. I wanted to start spending more time at home. At this point my business was thriving, and I was putting in a lot of hours, around eighty a week. Working at home had the advantage of being there for my family, but the disadvantage was working a lot more. I was working six to seven days a week. But I felt good about it, because I was home. It gave my husband a break from the kids too. He loved to golf and was on a baseball team since he was a kid. So he was able to enjoy what he loved to do. Everyone needs time to themselves, including me.

My husband went golfing once a week, and he played baseball once a week. So I decided to start going to Atlantic City once a week. I usually went on Thursday nights, after the kids went to bed. I only lived about an hour and fifteen minutes away, so I would get there between 11:00 p.m. and midnight. I would take a few hundred dollars with me, and if I lost it, I would go home. If I won, I would stay until I got tired, usually by 7 a.m. But for the most part, I would walk away a winner. I would always play this one slot machine before I left, and I would always hit something, anywhere from a few hundred to a few thousand dollars.

About six months into my weekly trips, I was tired and decided I didn't want to go. I even put my pajamas on and was going to go to bed early. At about 9:00 p.m., I got this overwhelming feeling. It was so strong, like nothing I had ever experienced. I told my husband that I had to go to Atlantic City. He thought I was crazy, but I told him I didn't know why, but I had to go. I got there at 10:30 p.m. that night. I did my usual and played the same slots I always did. I went down with five hundred dollars, and at 6:00 a.m., I still had three hundred dollars left. I was getting tired and wanted to go home. But, if you remember, I always played this one machine before I left. Well, for some reason, I paced in front of that machine for fifteen minutes, trying to decide whether to play it or walk away with my three hundred dollars. Since I am a risk taker, I said to myself, *What the heck. Something strong told me to come here, and if I don't do my normal routine, I might not ever find out why.*

I stood in front of my favorite slot machine and put a hundred dollars in it. I played it out, and nothing. I put the second hundred in, and still nothing. So I thought, *Here goes my last hundred.* I put it in and was down to thirty-eight dollars on the machine, and I looked away for a second as I pressed the button. I looked back at the machine, and one jackpot symbol came up, then a second one, then the third. All the lights went out for about a minute. I thought the machine had a malfunction. Then the light came back on, the sirens went off, and I was surrounded by people. I couldn't believe it; I had hit the jackpot. It was $4.3 million!

I was surrounded by the staff, onlookers, the media, and, of course, security. It was Friday, July 16, 2004. What a rush! It was unbelievable. I had to wait for all the paperwork to be done, and the media wanted to interview me. I got my big check and did my interview. I called my husband and told him to call our families. Of course, no one could believe it. God truly works in mysterious ways. It would turn out to be the best, and, yes, the worst day of my life.

When I got home, my husband actually had tears in his eyes. He said to me, "I am so happy for you. Now you won't have to work so hard."

Rings and Shackles

I told him that I was still keeping my business and would continue to work. This was going to help both our families. When I won the money, I honestly thought about how I would help everyone else. It took about a month to get my check. Because I took it as a lump sum, I got $2.7 million before taxes. After taxes, I got $1.4 million. But it was still more than anyone I knew had, and it was enough to take care of everyone.

The first thing I did was go to the bank to deposit the check and ask for cashier's checks made payable to family members. Then I told them I wanted $10,000 in cash to throw on my bed and roll in it. I went back home, and my kids and husband came into my bedroom. My son was six, and my daughter was now twelve. My son sat on my bed and asked to see the ten thousand. I threw it on the bed, and he rolled all over it. Then he sat there playing with it for the next hour. I told both my kids that they had a thousand dollars each to spend on whatever they wanted. You can imagine how happy they were. Then I called my brother and told him to come over, and I called my husband's family to let them know I was mailing them a check. They lived Upstate, so it was too far to come over.

Everyone was so happy, especially me. It was so nice to do this for both families. Everyone needed the money so badly too. Then I made a donation to two clients that were nonprofits and a donation to cancer research.

In October 2004, I started again with some health issues. I started hemorrhaging and had to go to the hospital. My doctor did a D&C and told me if it didn't work this time, I should consider a hysterectomy. Well, it didn't work, and I hemorrhaged again. So I went in for the hysterectomy. It had to be one of the most painful recoveries I ever went through. Stomach surgery is the worst to recover from. It took the full six weeks to recover. But, on the other hand, it was also the best surgery I had. No more periods!

It was now December 2004; I had just turned forty-four. We celebrated Christmas at my brother's, just as we did every year. It was really a beautiful Christmas. We had a lot to celebrate and be grateful for. I felt good, and everyone was so happy. After the holidays, it was time for my annual mammography. I went in just like I did each year since I was forty. After a few days, the radiologist called me to come back and have another one done. That was the first time I had to. So I went back, and I needed a biopsy.

On February 14, 2005, I got the most devastating news anyone could imagine. The radiologist called me and said, "I am sorry, but you have breast cancer."

I couldn't believe my ears. She told me what my next steps were, and after hanging up the phone, I just sat there in disbelief. My husband was next to me, and I just started crying and saying, "When does it all end?" We called and told both our families, and no one really knew what to say. I knew how everyone felt, especially my family. I also knew no matter what, my family would be there for me.

Shortly after being diagnosed with breast cancer, I went to my surgeon, the same one who took care of my melanoma. I had a partial mastectomy/lumpectomy followed by radiation and tamoxifen. The procedure needed before the surgery was actually more painful than the surgery itself. I had to be awake for this procedure. All women who have had mammograms know the pain of having your breast put in a vice until they are flat as a pancake. Well, in the procedure before my surgery, they put my left breast in the vice and put a needle in it to guide a wire to where the marker was placed during biopsy. The radiologist who did this put it in the wrong spot, and it had to be done again. I sat there for forty-five minutes while my breast was in a vice.

The surgery went well, and so did the recovery. Shortly after, I had to do the radiation. Months before being diagnosed, my whole family had scheduled a trip to Florida. I had a choice of doing the radiation before the trip or after. My husband and I met with my oncology radiologist, and we discussed all my options. They had a new procedure called "target radiation," which meant focusing on only where the cancer was and not the whole breast. I was supposed to do this for the next five weeks, but because I wanted it done before our trip to Florida, we did it twice a day for the next five days. I stayed at my brother's house near the hospital, and I went every morning and afternoon until I finished.

During this devastating time in my life, my husband's mother was diagnosed with lung cancer. My husband really wasn't good at handling bad news. His way of dealing with it was by not dealing with it. If all of this wasn't bad enough, he spiraled backward. I went through most of my radiation alone while he was out golfing and playing ball. I couldn't even comprehend how he could do this, especially when I needed him most. I couldn't even deal with him at this point, because I knew I needed to be strong for my children. So that's what I did, and when I finished my fifth day, the next morning we went to Florida.

Oh, Florida—better known as the trip from hell! First off, it was a trip for the kids. The weather was over 100 degrees the whole time we were there. I wasn't supposed to be exposed to the sun after my radiation, but the trip was already booked, and I didn't want to disappoint my children or my family. My husband, on the hand, turned out to be a big disappointment to us all. It was all about him. He just had to bring his golf clubs, because God forbid he did an unselfish act.

So while he and my brother went golfing every morning, I sat by the pool under an umbrella watching the kids. When they came back, we would go out to dinner and then see the sights or shows. I was so exhausted from my treatments, but I went all day and night to make everyone else happy. I didn't even complain. I just did what I had to, and I wish he would have done the same. He complained about everything when he wasn't golfing, such as it was too hot, there were too many people, and whatever else he could think of.

Rings and Shackles

After arriving back home from Florida, I was so disgusted and wiped out. The doctors told me radiation would make me exhausted, and it did. They had also put me on tamoxifen, which took some adjusting. After being diagnosed with breast cancer and going through what I did, it changed the way I thought about life. Winning the money and getting breast cancer also changed the way my husband thought about everything. Most married people would become closer, more supportive. He became distant and selfish.

When I won the money, I still kept all my clients. When I got sick, I had to give a lot of them up, but I still kept my business. I kept the ones I could do from my home office, allowing me to spend more time at home. It was a good thing for the kids and me, but it would turn out to be the worst for my husband and me. Now that I was home all the time, it put a damper on his daily activities. We started fighting all the time. His addiction took over, and he spent less time at home and more time playing baseball and going golfing. Whenever I confronted him about it, we would fight, and he would disappear Upstate to his family for days or weeks at a time. I would take him back every time too, because I had already gone through two marriages and I didn't want to give up on a third.

Over the next year, we fought about everything. He was out of control. He would complain every day about how much money I had given my family. The money was now a huge factor. He would harass me all the time for money. I even set him up in his own business, buying him a truck, tools, and whatever else he needed. I managed it for him, handling his customers and setting up and scouting for new ones, and I also did all of his accounting and paperwork. All he had to do was show up. But even that became too difficult for him. Customers would call me complaining, and my husband always had an answer for everything. One day he got lost, and he turned around and came back home. Every day got worse than the other. I was willing to keep doing it, but he just gave up. He couldn't handle dealing with people, and that included me.

There was no talking to him about anything. He never even wanted to be home anymore. I told him that every time he hurt me, it became easier to love him less. It really did. During 2006, we had redone the house right down to the studs. We redid the backyard and put in a pool for the kids. I bought myself some jewelry, a new SUV, and clothes. My house turned out beautiful, but it was at a huge price—not just financially, but mentally, physically, and every way you can think of. My husband and I did most of the work, with the exception of when he couldn't take it. He would just leave whatever he was doing to do his thing. It got to a point where I got so sick of him leaving that I just started throwing him out. I had to hire people to do things, only for them to rob me. You just can't trust anyone, and it's really sad. They would actually physically take things from my house. Of course, I fired them. What an ordeal. They were supposed to be my friends. They knew everything I was going through and still found it necessary to steal from me.

My marriage just got worse, and I loved him less and less. His family started hating me more and more from all the lies he was telling them. I even called his mother to try and talk to her, telling her there was something seriously wrong with him.

"Mom, I need your help. Your son is out of control, and I just don't know what to do anymore. Has he ever been diagnosed with a mental disorder?"

"Yes, Kim, he was as a kid. The doctors wanted him on medicine, but we didn't do it."

"Why? Maybe if he was, he wouldn't be like this."

"I'm sorry Kim, but you guys have to work out your own problems. I'm not getting involved." Then she hung up on me. That would explain a lot, such as his constant mood swings, depression, and being angry one minute and happy the next. His way of dealing with it for so many years was alcohol or substance abuse.

I then sat down with my husband to talk. "Listen, I really think you need to seek professional help. I will go with you so we can find out what's wrong."

"Kim, I'm not going to some quack, and there's nothing wrong with me."

"Your behavior is not normal. You need to see a doctor. I love you, but I can't take it anymore. If you don't go, I'm not going through this anymore."

So we went, and the doctor told us he was bipolar and needed to be medicated and to continue therapy. That didn't last too long, just like everything else he had done.

During 2006, things just kept getting worse. We had the police at our house all the time, and we spent so much money for lawyers going back and forth to court. Everything was over money, substance abuse, not wanting to be home, and the mood swings. It got to a point that even his family wasn't happy with how much money I gave them. It just wasn't enough. Everybody wanted more. Money is the root of all evil. I couldn't even enjoy my own money; they all sucked it out of me. I had already gave away half of what I got and decided the best thing to do was put the rest into my house. That way, when I retired, I would sell the house at a huge profit and have money to enjoy the rest of my life.

If all of that wasn't enough, it was September 2006 and time for my six-month mammography and MRI. Because I am a breast cancer patient, my doctor always requests a diagnostic mammogram. That way there is no waiting for results. I get the results right then and there.

Well, here it was, only a year and half later from my original diagnosis, and yet again, there was more bad news. This time there was abnormal growth in both breasts. The diagnosis was ductal atypical hyperplasia. There were so many abnormal cells that a normal biopsy wouldn't suffice. So I went to see my surgeon again, and we scheduled the surgery.

It was the night before my surgery, and my husband, my kids, and I were sitting at the kitchen table having dinner. Out of nowhere, my husband yells at my daughter. "Feed the cats!"

"I will feed them when I'm done eating."

My husband wasn't satisfied with the answer and started arguing with my daughter over cat food. I was going back in the hospital again, and he was worried about cat food. So we started arguing, and he got up and went in the den.

My husband decided to call his mother. "Mom, I've had enough. I'm leaving her and taking my son with me. I can't take it anymore."

Ah, life was so hard for him. The man lived like a king. He didn't have to work, played golf two to three times a week, baseball one to two times a week, and got high whenever he wanted. But he couldn't take it anymore.

I got up, went into the den, stood in the doorway, waited for him to get off the phone with his mother, and then I said very calmly, "You are right. You are done. Only because I said you're done. You are leaving, and leaving without our son. Over my dead body will you ever take my son away from me. Now you can take your belongings and leave."

Not one tear did I shed. As he sat there cursing me out, I walked away and started cleaning up and packing for me and the kids. The phone rang, and it was my sister-in-law. She wanted to see how I was doing and to find out what time I was leaving. She was taking care of my kids, just like she always did during my surgery. We were all going to stay there during my recovery.

During my conversation, my husband came out of the den and went into my purse.

"What are you doing?" I asked.

"I'm taking your debit card," he said. "I need money."

"Kim, what's going on?" my sister-in-law asked.

"He's taking my bank card and won't give it back."

"Are you kidding me?"

"Nope, and he's cursing me out."

My brother heard our conversation and told my sister-in-law to give him the phone. "Kim, put your husband on the phone now."

So I did, and I will never forget the look on his face or his frantic pacing back and forth. He told him that if he didn't leave the house now, give me back my card, and stop it, he would be on his way to my house. Now if you knew my brother, you would understand the panic in my husband. He left and went Upstate to his family, and shortly after, I went to mine.

The next morning my brother took me to the hospital while my sister-in-law watched my kids. Even though my brother was with me, it was hard because he couldn't come in with me, nor did I want him to. So here I went again. Only this time it was both breasts.

So there I was, standing there while the radiologist and her assistant were doing this procedure, and all of a sudden, the tears just started rolling down my face uncontrollably. They kept asking me, "Are you okay? Do you want us to stop? Is it too painful? What's wrong?" But I just couldn't stop crying. A little while after that, I was able to pull myself together. "I'm sorry, my husband and I just separated because he couldn't handle it anymore." Truthfully, I wasn't crying over the fact that we weren't together anymore. After everything I went through, he couldn't handle it. Wow!

I went up for surgery. It took about five hours, and then I was in recovery for a couple of more hours. My brother came in and stayed with me until it was time to go. We went home to his house. I wasn't feeling too bad from this one, but of course, I didn't see the results of it yet either. It would be a couple of more days before I would see what was done. I needed two more lumpectomies/partial mastectomies. The worst part was the atypical hyperplasia that was on my left breast was so big, and I didn't know how big until I took the bandage off.

My sister-in-law and I were in her bathroom, and I asked her to help me take them off. We started with the right breast, which wasn't too bad. I lost part of the top of it. Then we went on to the left breast, and when we took off the bandages, I just started crying. I had lost half of it, and it had a large indentation. I was so upset. I can't even begin to tell you how devastated I was. I couldn't stop sobbing. There I was, without my beautiful breast anymore. I looked and felt like a dissected pig. My sister-in-law tried cheering me up by saying it wasn't that bad and then showed me hers. She said, "How would you like to have these?"

We both started laughing. It was cute and sweet, but it would take me a long time to feel good about myself again. After the surgery, I had to continue every six months of mammograms, MRIs, and blood work. My blood counts were low, and I needed IV treatments for my iron.

We stayed at my brother's during the week for the next month, and we went home on the weekends. My husband was still Upstate, but he kept calling. I didn't talk to him until I was ready. When I finally did talk to him, this is what transpired:

"Kim, I'm so sorry. I love you and just want to come home."

"I know you're sorry, just like always. But for me it's too late. Nothing you say could ever take away what you have done. Our marriage ended the night before my surgery, and to be honest, it was a relief. With everything I have been through, I can't even think about dealing with you anymore." I felt free for the first time in ten years.

I was alone with my two children, and my family wanted me to move back to Staten Island to be close to them. I didn't want to move back because I had put so much money into my house and I finally had my dream home. But my family made a lot of sense. They kept telling me that because of my health and being a single mom, they would help me. They would be there for me mentally and physically, and there was nothing left for me in New Jersey. They were right. What did I have? Only my dream house. It was a material thing. It was more important to be by my family.

I put my house up for sale. In the meantime, I no longer had any money to live and had to borrow from family and friends. I am still trying to pay it back. It became a nightmare. It was right when the housing market crashed and nothing was selling. It was horrible, and I had to take a huge loss. So I started looking through the papers for a house to rent on Staten Island. It took a few weeks, but I found one right down the street from my brother. How convenient was that? I was picking up the pieces again.

Single Mom for the First Time: Shoot Me Please If I Ever Get Married Again

Staten Island, New York

I moved back to Staten Island as a single mom with two kids, but the best part was that I was close to my family. It was very hard at first, because once again, I was starting over and I had never rented before. I always owned my homes, and now I had to deal with a landlord and paying rent and putting money in someone else's pocket. But what was I going to do? I really didn't have much of choice. I also had to either build my business back up or just get a full-time job. So I started looking through the papers and went online every day. I sent out over one thousand résumés. Yes, really. A few months later, I started getting responses. I ended up taking on a few new clients, and one of them needed me full time. I became his chief financial officer, and the rest I did at night or on the weekends.

Now you may be wondering what happened to my husband. After living Upstate for about six months, he started calling me.

"I want you back, Kim. I want my family back."

"I'm sorry, but I can't take you back. You had ten years to get it right and didn't. I'm not going through that again. I moved on and so should you."

"But I will change. I promise."

"I have heard that story so many times, and I'm sorry. It's too late."

The truth finally hit him, and he couldn't handle it. The phone calls became more depressing.

After I moved back to Staten Island, I filed for divorce. He was devastated knowing that I had finally had enough. He couldn't believe I wouldn't take him back, and neither could anyone else. I had done it so many times before, but this time was different for me. He wasn't there for me in my darkest hour, and what he said had ended it for me. I would never feel the same about him.

Because my soon-to-be ex-husband was going into a deep depression, I agreed to help him. He wanted to move back to Staten Island to be closer to us, so I told him he could stay with us until he found a place to live. I also told him we weren't getting back together but I would help him. What can I say? That's who I am. I have always helped people throughout my life and would even give the shirt off my back if I had to. Besides, he was the father of my son, and I wanted him to be around to see his son grow up.

Once he knew I was willing to help him, he left Upstate and came to my house. I let him stay on the couch and told him we would start looking for doctors immediately and he was going to get the help he had needed for such a long time. He admitted to me for the first time that he did have problems and wanted the help. But he couldn't do it without me.

The next day, we got in touch with the right doctors, and for the next few months, I went back and forth with him. He was diagnosed as bipolar and put on the right medication to help him. At first he was doing great and doing all the right things. He even moved out of my house and in with a relative. He wasn't eating right, so I let him come over to have dinner with us each night. That way he would have time with the kids too. I know he needed to feel part of something, especially our lives.

This went on for quite some time. My family, of course, didn't understand how I could even help him, but I told them to please let me handle it in my own way. So that's what they did. I still cared about him, even though I wasn't in love with him anymore. As much as I had suffered over the years, I still couldn't let him suffer. Some people just can't handle it, and others are just born to be fighters. I am one of those people: a born fighter. How else could I explain my survival?

Well, just like every other thing my ex-husband ever started, this came to a halt. Because he started feeling better, he felt he didn't need the help anymore.

I said, "What about doing it for yourself and your son?" But he thought it was going to get us back together, so why bother?

This man had been this way his whole life, and no matter what I did, I knew he wouldn't change. He had to want it bad enough himself and he just never did, even at the cost of losing his family. So I moved forward with my life, doing what I had to, and we remained friends—even more than friends. He's a man, and I'm a woman; we both had needs. So for the next three and a half years, we fulfilled each other's needs, and that was it. It was easier for both of us. Neither one of us wanted to go through the dating thing and another relationship. I also didn't want to bring someone into the mess I was dealing with.

I don't know what happened, but after three and a half years of this, it finally hit me: *What the hell am I doing?* I just couldn't do it anymore. I was still dealing with the same man who refused to change for me or our family, and it just made me sick inside. I couldn't do it anymore, nor did I want to. I didn't love him that way anymore, and it just didn't feel right at all. So I told him I just couldn't do it anymore. Well, of course, he didn't take it well. He became so bitter and angry, and he wasn't nice about it. But I knew I had to end it for good, no matter what the outcome. I needed to move on with my life, and so did he. So that's what we did. It wasn't easy, but of course, I helped him through it, letting him know I would always care about him and be his friend.

After three failed marriages, I figured marriage just wasn't for me and that I would be single for the rest of my life. I didn't think I would ever find true love, and I was better off being alone. So I concentrated on my work and my children. My daughter and my family kept trying to get me to go out and meet someone, but at forty-nine years old, I just couldn't do it anymore. Relationships were just too hard, and I felt like I put everything I had into it and didn't get the same in return.

During all this time, I kept up with my doctors and tests every six months. After four years of being stable, I went for my six-month checkup, and there were more abnormal cells growing and multiplying. They put me back into high risk again and said we needed to keep a close eye on it. Any more changes and I would need to discuss further options.

Fourth Marriage:
So Get Out the Gun and Shoot Me

I was doing exactly what I said I would. I was minding my own business and concentrating on my work and my children until one day, four months after telling my ex-husband we needed to part ways, while at work, I went outside. This man from the business next door came up and started talking to me.

"My name is Michael. What's yours?"

"Kim. I see you're a bus driver."

"Yep, I drive motor coaches."

"Nice, I'm the CFO."

"Kim, can I see your left hand?"

"Sure, Michael, and nope, I'm not married. How about you?"

Nope, it's just me and my son. He's two, and I have been fighting for custody since he was born" What he went through, and what his son was put through, really touched me.

He then asked me, "What does a man have to do to go on a date with you?"

I replied, "Have a job and be a man, not a child. I already have two kids."

So he pointed to the bus he was driving and said, "I have a job."

We exchanged business cards and parted ways.

When I went inside, I told everyone at work, and they were so happy and telling me I should go on a date if he asked.

I said, "I don't know. I haven't been on a date in fourteen years."

A few hours later, he called me. I was surprised he called me so soon. He said some really nice things, and we had a good conversation. Over the next few weeks, we talked a few times and sent e-mails back and forth. He was a charter bus driver and traveled a lot. I worked a lot and had two kids. He lived in Philadelphia, and I lived in Staten Island. I felt like it would be too much work on both parts to have a long-distance relationship. Even though it was a two-hour driving distance, which really isn't that far, I felt it was too far for me. So I sent him an e-mail telling him how nice of guy he was but, with our work schedules and busy lives, I didn't think it would work.

He didn't respond to my e-mail, and a couple of days later, he called me. He said he got my e-mail and to please just give him a chance and I wouldn't be disappointed. He would be so good to me that I wouldn't want to be without him. What a line, right?

I told him, "I don't know. I will think about it."

So that's what I did; I thought about it for a couple of days. When I was on the phone that night, he told me he was doing a charter and would be in New York on Friday. I thought about it right up until Friday night when I got home from work. I couldn't stop thinking about it. I talked to my family, and they told me to go and that I deserved to be happy. If I didn't go, I would never know.

So I called him and said, "I'm about to make your night."

He was so happy, saying, "Really? Are you serious?"

"Yep, tell me the time and place."

So we met up in New Jersey, where his charter group was staying for the night. When I got there, I parked my car and watched him unload the bus.

I called him and told him, "Stop unloading and come say hello to me."

He came up to my car with a huge smile on his face, and he leaned in and kissed me. He parked the bus, and we went inside to his room. I sat on the chair while he got changed. He came and sat on an ottoman in front of the chair I was sitting on. He reached into his bag and pulled out a dozen pink roses. He picked pink because of my breast cancer. That really touched me in a way I hadn't felt in a very long time. I couldn't believe he remembered from our previous conversations. We had such a great time, and

I was so happy I went. The happiness I felt that night was something I thought I would never feel again.

We spent the next couple of months taking turns commuting back and forth a couple times a week. When we weren't together, we were on the phone for hours. It got to the point where we didn't want to be apart. He did something for me that no man had done in a long time: he made me laugh. I felt alive again. I met and fell in love with his son too. We all became close, and we both felt the same about each other. We didn't want to be apart anymore.

He asked me to marry him, and to my surprise, I truly wanted to. It felt so right. I know it wasn't that long, but we really loved each other. It felt like we had known each other forever. So we got engaged and moved in together. He gained custody of his son in August 2010, and they both moved to Staten Island.

My children had a little bit of a hard time accepting him and his son, but they eventually grew on each other. It was an adjustment for everyone. My children and my stepson now refer to each other as brothers and sister. Since moving in with us, for the first time in his little life, my stepson has a stable environment, a family life, loves school, and is just so healthy and happy. He always refers to all of us as his family, with a big smile.

We set our wedding date in December 2010. I wanted to get married before my next doctor's appointment. If I needed surgery or treatments, I wanted my husband by my side. We were originally going to get married in the Poconos but decided not to. We decided to have the wedding in Philly at his grandmother's house. We had a small, simple wedding surrounded by family and friends. It was beautiful and one of the happiest days of my life.

It was now time again for my tests. The results were what I expected: not good. There was new abnormal growth. I met with my doctors, and they once again gave me my options. I told them I was ready. After six years of everything, I was finally ready. So we scheduled my surgery for March 9, 2011. I had put it off long enough. I talked to my full-time client, where I was the chief financial officer, and he agreed to pay me while I was out of work. I knew that was one more thing I didn't have to worry about during my recovery time.

The day before my surgery, I needed to go to the hospital and have dye injected into my lymph nodes. If anyone out there has ever had this done, you know I was about to find out that this would be the most painful procedure I would ever go through. I had to be awake for it, and they gave me a couple of needles in each breast to numb the area. Well, it didn't numb anything. Then they had to inject four needles into each nipple, one right after the other—eight in all. It was the most painful experience of my life. The tears were just rolling down my face. Nipples have so many nerves and sensation that the needles were excruciating. After they were done, I went through a scan to make sure the dye went to my lymph nodes. Thank God it worked, because I couldn't have gone through it again without being knocked out.

My surgery was scheduled for 7 a.m., and we had to be there two hours before. My husband was right by my side. They took me in for prepping, and he stayed with me until I went in. I went in to have a nipple-sparing bilateral mastectomy with a tram flap. This was the only surgery I could have. I couldn't have implants because I had already had radiation in my left breast. If I had implants, scar tissue would develop from the radiation, and I would need to have surgery again. My husband was in the waiting room the whole fifteen hours of my surgery. He said he came into recovery and sat with me for the five minutes they let him. He said I was out of it. They had me on so much pain medication that I didn't wake up until the next day.

The next day I woke up in the intensive care unit, where I spent the next seven days. I could only have visitors three times a day for a half hour each time. Everyone came to see me the next day, and the good news was that my lymph nodes were clear—no cancer. Everyone was so happy, including me. The next seven days were extremely painful for me, and I didn't know it then, but I found out that my nipple-sparing mastectomy was unsuccessful. My nipples died during the surgery, and I lost them.

For anyone who doesn't know what type of surgery I had, allow me to explain it. My doctors took out all of my breast tissue, leaving only the outer skin. They opened my stomach from hip to hip and took muscle, fatty tissue, and blood vessels to form my breasts. Then they reattached the vessels in my breasts for the blood supply.

After the seven days in ICU, I was transferred to a regular room. The great part about that was everyone being able to visit me. I thought my hysterectomy recovery was bad; boy, oh boy, I have to say that this was the worst ever. After another week, I was able to go home. I needed a nurse to come to the house, because I was a mess. I had tubes coming out of both my breasts and stomach for drainage. A few days later, I went to my doctors for my checkup, and he took out the tubes. I didn't need the nurse anymore, and I had the help of my daughter and sister-in-law.

My original recovery was supposed to be six to eight weeks. I didn't think I would ever recover. I had to clean the surgical areas and change the bandages twice a day. It was absolutely awful. The pain was unbelievable; it kept me up all night. Even with painkillers, it was so hard to move or be pain-free.

After being home for two weeks, in the middle of the night while I was in bed, I woke up all wet on the right side of my stomach. I figured I just had some drainage, but the next morning, my sister-in-law came over, and I told her what happened. Then, out of the blue, I got the chills and had a fever. We called my doctor, and he told us to go to my regular doctor. He felt I might have the flu. So that's what we did. My doctor sent me for a chest X-ray, which was fine, and gave me antibiotics.

At around 11:00 p.m. that night, I still wasn't feeling well, and my temperature went up to 102. I was still draining a little, and I opened my bandage on my stomach. The surgical site was turning red and was swollen, with yellow puss. I had my daughter look at it, and she said it didn't look good. So we called my sister-in-law to take me to the emergency room. When we got there, they took me right in. I had a very bad infection and had to be readmitted. I spent another week in the hospital on IV antibiotics. In a really short period of time, the infection spread through my whole stomach and even into my breasts. It was horrible and looked even worse. I spent the next three weeks cleaning and putting medicine on twice a day again until it finally started healing.

It was now nine weeks after my surgery, and I was finally starting to feel like a normal person again. I had a follow-up appointment with my surgeon, which turned out much better than I expected.

After examining me, he said, "So when do you want to have your next surgery?"

I was very pleased, because, with the infection and all, we thought it would be a lot longer. So we scheduled my next surgery for June 30, 2011. This one was same-day surgery, and

I would leave the hospital having nipples. The recovery was about a month, and then I would have my last procedure: the medical tattooing of the areola. This is the area around the nipples. I would be done sometime in July 2011.

In the meantime, I went back to work part time. I was supposed to be paid while I was out. During those nine weeks, I received very little due to the financial situation of the business. So I spoke to the owner.

"I will work part time until my next surgery, but I need to get at least half of my pay just to cover my bills."

"Kim, I can't promise you half, but I will do the best I can. Whatever comes in during the week will be split with everyone working."

"Okay, that's fair, especially if no one was paid while I was out. But if I find out that everyone got paid and I didn't, I'm not going to be happy."

Now remember, I was the chief financial officer for this client. Knowing that, wouldn't I find out whether or not people were paid? I truly don't understand the way people think. If you knew all the things I did for this man and his business, I'm sure you would feel the same way. The first week I went back, I got no pay, and neither did anyone else. The second week I got a small fraction of my normal pay, and so did everyone else. The third week I was entering the payroll from when I was out, and guess what. To my total and complete disgust, everyone except me got paid the whole time I was out. Isn't that nice? So naturally, I marched right into the owner's office.

"You lied to me and left me hanging during my absence while everyone else got paid. How could you do this to me? I worked so hard and gave up so much for you, and for what? Only to be gone and forgotten about. Nothing you could say can make up for what you did to me."

I finished out my day, with neither of us talking to each other, and then I went home, never to return. I haven't talked to him since, nor do I care to. What a disappointment. He was supposed to be my friend too. Well, friends don't stab you in the back. They look out for each other. Way to go, great looking out for me. So here I am again, picking up the pieces.

It was now June 2011, and I went in for my nipple surgery. Everything went well. It took longer than expected to heal. Another three months went by, and it was time for my areola tattooing. So in September, I went in for my final surgery. The surgery was a success. Now I have to see my doctors every six months to make sure there are no changes. When the doctors are comfortable with my progress, I will continue to see them on an annual basis.

Since then, I have picked up a couple of new clients. Actually, one is an old one who needed my help again. So I am working part time again, which is perfect. I have time for my son and stepson. My daughter got engaged Christmas 2011. She moved into an apartment with her finance. My husband and I just celebrated our first anniversary. Life is wonderful!

Conclusion

I am now fifty-one years old, married for the fourth time, and living back on Staten Island. Is this the end? No, of course not. This is a new beginning for me. I will continue to survive, because that is just who I am: a true fighter. I will continue to fight, and I will never give up. Everyone has problems, and you need to take whatever life throws at you, one day at a time. Do the best you can, pray a lot, and move on. In the end, you only have one person to answer to. Life goes on, hold your head up high, and know that whatever happens, you did the best you could. I know I have, and through everything, I have no regrets. What the future holds for me, who knows? But I do know this: I will continue picking up the pieces, and you can too.